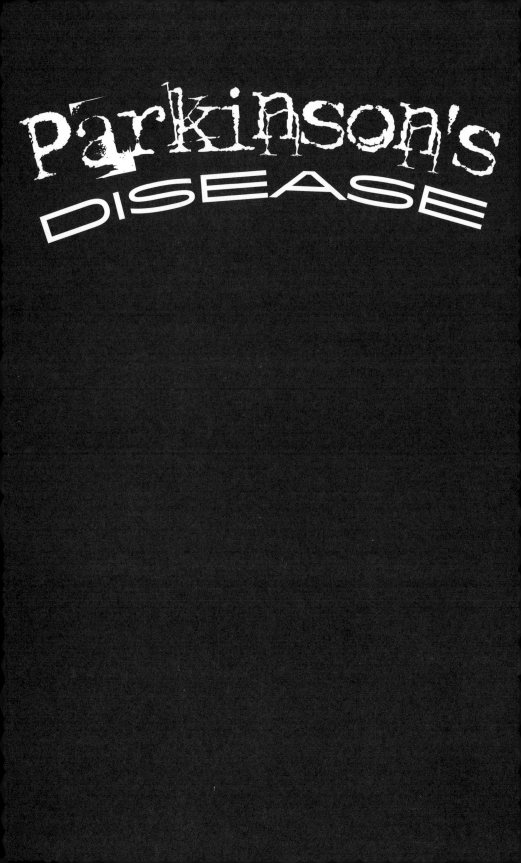

Parkinson's DISEASE

Parkinson's DISEASE

ELAINE LANDAU

A Venture Book

Franklin Watts
A Division of Grolier Publishing
New York / London / Hong Kong / Sydney
Danbury, Connecticut

Photographs ©: Ben Klaffke: 12, 41, 45, 53, 79, 82, 85, 90; Corbis-Bettmann: 17 (Omar Torres/AFP); Gamma-Liaison: 19 (Schwarzwald); National Institute of Neurological Disorders and Stroke: 36 (National Institues of Health, Bethesda, MD); Photo Researchers: cover, 3 (Scott Camazine), 65 (Fred Lombardi), 58 (SIU).

Visit Franklin Watts on the Internet at:
http://publishing.grolier.com

Interior design by Joan M. McEvoy

Library of Congress Cataloging-in-Publication Data

Landau, Elaine.
    Parkinson's disease / Elaine Landau.
        p. cm. — (Venture)
    Includes bibliographical references and index.
    Summary: Introduces Parkinson's disease, a nerve disorder that often causes uncontrollable shaking and loss of energy in its victims.
    ISBN 0-531-11423-6
    1. Parkinson's disease—Juvenile literature. [1. Parkinson's disease.] I. Title.
    RC382.L36 1999
    616.8'33—dc21   98-22450
                                         CIP
                                         AC

GROLIER Printed in the United States of America
PUBLISHING 1 2 3 4 5 6 7 8 9 10 R 08 07 06 05 04 03 02 01 00 99

Contents

CHAPTER 1

Parkinson's Disease

Frank R.

For several years, Frank R., a cartoonist for a Chicago newspaper, had eagerly looked forward to his retirement. The summer before he left his job, Frank and his wife Barbara bought a cabin in the beautiful mountains of Colorado where they had enjoyed many summer vacations. Frank and Barbara planned to spend their days fishing and sailing on the crystal-clear lakes and hiking and biking on scenic trails.

However, within a year of moving to Colorado, the couple realized that their retirement might not be what they had planned. For the first time in his life, Frank felt his health was failing. The flu-like symptoms had come on slowly and Frank had felt achy and stiff. But it wasn't the flu, and as time passed the mysterious soreness continued.

Frank had other symptoms too. Although he cut back on his activities, he was always feeling tired. He had no energy and he noticed it took him longer to do things. In the past, he'd found sailing relaxing, but taking his boat out exhausted him now. Frank was afraid that something was very wrong, but he nevertheless put off seeing a doctor.

Jessica P.

As a young woman, Jessica P. was a professional dancer and in later years ran a girls' jazz and ballet school. She had always considered herself strong and athletic so she was puzzled when she developed a tremor in her left hand. Sometimes, when she least expected it, her hand would begin to shake and tremble as though it were unconnected to her body. It was especially upsetting that the tremor frequently occurred when she was speaking to a class of young dancers. It didn't take long for Jessica to realize that her students were looking at her shaking hand rather than listening to what she was saying.

Like Frank R., Jessica P. often felt stiff and sore. At times her joints ached so badly that she had to ask another instructor to demonstrate dance steps to her students. Jessica also felt that her movements were no longer quick or graceful and that her body was increasingly rigid. And it was obvious to her—and everyone around her—that she was moving much more slowly.

Within the last few months, Jessica had to concentrate to complete even routine tasks. Now she had to think carefully about executing simple dance steps she had done since childhood. What once came so naturally was now a major effort. She didn't know what was happening to her, but she knew she didn't like it.

Richard J.

Richard J., a retired engineer, had many of the same symptoms as Frank R. and Jessica P. He felt his body stiffen and noticed he moved slower than before. What Richard didn't realize was that he had begun to drag his left foot and had developed a slight limp. When Richard's wife first remarked on this, he said she was imagining it. But when she showed him the worn-down side of his left shoe, he couldn't deny it any longer.

Richard's puzzling symptoms were as troubling to his grandchildren as they were to him. Every Christmas, Richard wrote each child a wonderful letter and enclosed it with a gift. The children cherished these letters and carefully pasted them in scrapbooks. They hoped to share them with their own children someday.

But last Christmas the letters looked different. Richard's messages were as meaningful and kind as before, but his handwriting was strange. He started out each sentence writing normally, but by the end of the line his writing became unusually small. It was as if he had no room to finish and tried to squeeze all he wanted to say into a few lines. Yet there was more than enough space on the page.

Communication between Richard J. and his grandchildren changed in other ways too. As they were growing up, the grandchildren had always been close to Richard. They felt comfortable telling him their secrets and often said that their grandfather knew their thoughts and feelings.

The young people believed that they knew their grandfather as well he knew them, but over the past year it had become nearly impossible for anyone to guess at Richard's feelings. He always seemed to have a blank look on his face now instead of the broad range of expressions that had once quickly revealed his opinions. It was hard to remember his lively imitations of Bugs Bunny and Donald Duck.

Although these three people don't know one another, they have something in common. Their symptoms are slightly different, but they all have an illness known as Parkinson's disease—or PD. Parkinson's disease is one of a number of conditions that affect bodily movement, so it is known as a motor system disorder. Its most common symptoms are described here.

Symptoms of Parkinson's Disease
TREMOR
The tremor associated with Parkinson's disease generally takes the form of trembling in the hands, arms, legs, jaw, and face. The tremor usually begins in the hand, but in some cases it first appears in the foot or

jaw. In about three-fourths of people with Parkinson's disease, the tremor begins on one side of the body. But more than one body part may be affected. Once the disease progresses, the tremor often spreads to other areas. In most people with PD, the tremor is worse when the affected body part is at rest or when the person is under stress. Although some PD patients find the tremor annoying or embarrassing, it is usually not severe enough to be disabling.

RIGIDITY

Rigidity, also described as stiffness, is experienced by most of those with Parkinson's disease. Due to the disturbance in signals from the brain that occurs in Parkinson's disease, the patient's muscles remain continually tensed, making them stiff and achy. Often experiencing what is known as "cogwheel" rigidity, these individuals move their limbs in short jerky movements.

SLOWNESS OF MOVEMENT

Slower movement as well as a loss of spontaneous action is frequently a telltale sign of PD. Technically known as *bradykinesia*, this symptom can be especially frustrating when patients are unable to carry out simple tasks quickly and easily.

Bradykinesia is also unpredictable. The person may wake up feeling limber but need help getting out of a chair by mid-morning. The individual has to concentrate on actions once done automatically, such as opening a door, running a bath, or tying a shoelace. Bradykinesia can dramatically alter a person's lifestyle. Some PD patients take several hours to wash and dress each morning.

One woman with Parkinson's disease described how bradykinesia affected her work performance:

> *"I was a 53-year-old woman and very energetic . . . I worked as a secretary in a commercial glass firm. One day . . . everything started being such a chore . . . Every time my boss asked me to get a record, it seemed I was down in the files for hours. Hours! My hands weren't working right, you know; as if they weren't my usual hands."*[1]

IMPAIRED POSTURE

Impaired or unstable posture affecting the person's balance and coordination is common among people with PD. Patients often develop a tendency to lean either forward or backward. At times, they topple over. Someone who once had excellent posture may now be stooped over with his or her shoulders drooped and head lowered. Patients who lean backward may also exhibit a symptom called retropulsion—if bumped from the front, they step backward.

Unfortunately, coordination tends to decrease as the disease advances. A person walking across a room may suddenly "freeze" in mid-stride. In such sit-

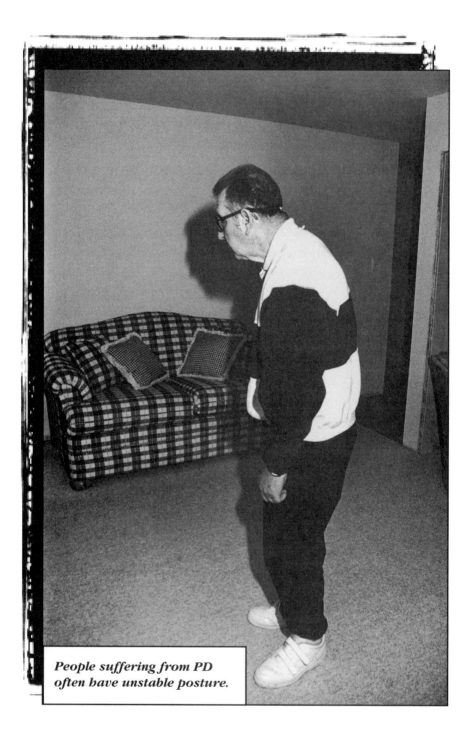

People suffering from PD often have unstable posture.

uations, the individual sometimes stumbles or falls. The coordination problems associated with Parkinson's disease take other forms as well. Patients often develop a shuffling gait. Yet it's not unusual to see someone with Parkinson's disease taking several short quick steps forward, as if trying to keep his or her balance. This type of quickening motion in Parkinson's patients is known as *festination*.

The "Shaking Palsy"—An Unsolved Puzzle

Parkinson's disease was first identified by an English physician named James Parkinson. Up to that time, the condition had been known as "the shaking" because of the tremors exhibited by those with the disease. In 1817, Dr. Parkinson published a paper entitled "The Shaking Palsy" in which he described PD's symptoms with amazing accuracy. During the next 150 years, medical scientists worked hard to learn more about the origin of the illness and possible treatments.

Researchers still don't know the precise cause of Parkinson's disease, but they have suggested a number of theories. Some think that PD may be brought on by environmental toxins. Supporters of this theory note that Parkinson's disease tends to be more prevalent in industrialized urban centers than in rural areas. When clusters of Parkinson's disease cases are identified in rural areas, there is often a chemical or industrial plant nearby. Some researchers further argue that the chemical MPTP causes a closely related illness called toxin-induced parkinsonism. Doctors became aware of this during the 1980s when numerous California heroin addicts exhibited PD-like symptoms after taking an illegal street drug containing MPTP.

Another theory is that Parkinson's disease is caused by a still unidentified virus. Following a 1916 flu epidemic that swept through the United States, a surprisingly large number of flu victims were left with symptoms resembling Parkinson's disease. Some researchers suspect that a connection exists.

A third explanation proposes that Parkinson's disease symptoms result from the unavoidable effects of the aging process on the brain. If this theory is correct, anyone who lives long enough would eventually have Parkinson's disease.

These are just a few of the theories that attempt to explain PD. Some scientists believe that most PD cases have both a genetic and an environmental basis.

To learn about a possible hereditary factor in Parkinson's disease, scientists studied twins. In some sets of identical twins only one got PD while in others both twins eventually developed the illness. However, it's difficult to identify a hereditary or genetic factor in an illness appearing so late in life. Adults, even identical twins, usually have a broad range of varied life experiences. By the time one or both are diagnosed with PD, each twin may have been exposed to numerous other possible causes for the disease.

The PD studies of twins did yield one interesting observation, however. One of the major differences between the twins who got Parkinson's and those who didn't, was that those who escaped the condition smoked more. Surprisingly, this unexpected finding was confirmed in subsequent studies. However, it is not recommended that people smoke to avoid PD. Smoking can result in lethal health problems leading to death long before an individual ever exhibits PD symptoms. Instead, researchers are now trying to learn more about smoking's preventive property as it might someday prove beneficial to PD patients in a safer form.

Meanwhile, further research on a possible genetic link in PD has continued. In the summer of 1997, National Institutes of Health (NIH) researchers announced an important breakthrough in identifying an abnormal gene responsible for some cases of PD. These scientists had discovered a tiny mistake in the gene that codes for a protein called alpha synuclein. Although the protein had not been previously connected to PD, this gene's abnormality seemed responsible for a small number of PD cases occurring within families. This fairly rare form of PD tends to strike somewhat earlier and progresses more rapidly.

The research group discovered the genetic link by studying a large southern Italian family and three parkinsonian families of Greek origin. In these groups, about half the children developed Parkinson's disease when one of their parents had the gene abnormality. Unfortunately, researchers still do not know precisely how this genetic abnormality eventually leads to PD's characteristic cell destruction.

So while this advance is important to PD research, it does not firmly establish a genetic link to Parkinson's disease for the majority of people who have the illness.

Further research is needed. Former world heavyweight champion Muhammad Ali, who has suffered from Parkinson's symptoms since the early 1980s has encouraged minorities to participate in Parkinson's disease research studies. On September 24, 1996, Ali and the pharmaceutical company Pharmacia & Upjohn announced the first Parkinson's disease study specifically centering on people of African, Asian, and Latin descent.

As Ali's wife Lonnie noted—"My husband has been battling Parkinson's for over a decade. I believe the time has come for us as a community to step into the ring and face Parkinson's disease."[2]

For now, researchers have learned a number of important facts about people who develop Parkinson's. PD knows no social, financial, or geographical limitations. It affects individuals of all races around the world, although it strikes more white people than blacks or Asians.

Parkinson's disease also largely affects older individuals. Before age sixty, more men than women suffer from PD, but the numbers even out after that. Yet while the illness is more common in people over sixty, some people develop Parkinson's disease in their forties and fifties. Scientists are not sure why, but this trend appears to be increasing. Cases of "early-onset" Parkinson's have been identi-

Muhammad Ali lights the torch at the Olympic Games, Atlanta, 1996.

fied in even younger patients. Some physicians report that 5 to 10 percent of their PD patients are under forty.

Among these is actor Michael J. Fox who was diagnosed with the disease in his early thirties. In 1991 while filming the movie "Doc Hollywood," Fox experienced a twitching sensation in his left pinkie. Over the years his symptoms intensified. In commenting on his illness, the actor's neurologist Dr. Allan Ropper noted that nothing in particular had made Fox susceptible to the disease and that his case didn't differ significantly from that of his other patients.

Contrary to public opinion, most medical researchers seriously doubt that an accident, injury, or shock could result in Parkinson's disease. Nevertheless, numerous lawsuits have been launched on this premise. Some individuals insist that they developed PD after hitting their head in a car accident two to three years earlier. Others wrongfully claim that their PD symptoms developed after being struck by a falling object. Parkinson's has also been wrongly attributed to brain surgery or the shock of traumatic news. However, thousands of people around the world have accidents, emotional upheavals, and surgery without getting Parkinson's disease.

Although its cause remains unknown, doctors today know how PD affects the brain and produces its classic symptoms. The problem centers around a chemical substance in the brain called *dopamine,* one of the brain's neurotransmitters. Like all neuro-

Michael J. Fox filming the hit T.V. series, "Spin City."

transmitters, dopamine carries messages between nerve cells. Dopamine also controls our physical movement and coordination.

The cells that fabricate the body's dopamine are located in a part of the brain known as the *substantia nigra.* From there, the dopamine travels to the *corpus striatum,* another part of the brain, where it helps regulate the body's muscles and movements.

For a variety of reasons, we all lose some dopamine-producing cells throughout our lives. However, we have so many that the loss isn't felt until a tremendous number of them are gone. Unfortunately, just such a loss occurs in individuals with PD. When a significant number of dopamine-producing cells in the substantia nigra are destroyed, less dopamine reaches the corpus striatum—and PD symptoms appear.

Although Parkinson's disease is debilitating, it is not fatal. Yet it is often difficult to predict the effect PD will have on a specific person's lifespan. PD does not follow a steady predictable course. Symptoms develop at different rates in different individuals. Therefore, two people diagnosed with PD at the same time will not necessarily have similar experiences in the years ahead. One may be seriously debilitated by the illness within the first ten years while another patient's symptoms can remain relatively slight for as long as twenty-five years.

Although Parkinson's is classified as a progressive disease (an illness that worsens with time), its symptoms aren't always a downward spiral. For no apparent reason, a patient's tremor may worsen and then improve, only to worsen again. As one patient said, "You never know. I thought my tremor had progressed to the point of my being unable to use my hand. Then it got a lot better. Why? I don't know. Parkinson's disease is like a roller coaster—you never know when you're going to go up or when you're going to go down."[3]

Thelma A., another PD patient, described the unpredictable nature of her illness:

> *"My condition has stabilized over the past years. I wouldn't say I've gotten any worse over the past seven years since I got the disease. In the first years I felt like I was falling down a well—things were getting so bad so fast. It was out of control. Then all of a sudden it seemed my symptoms stabilized and have stayed at that same plateau since, no better and no worse."[4]*

Parkinson's disease generally starts subtly. Early symptoms may be slight and develop gradually. In most cases, people begin to feel tired, or bit shaky on their feet. Some find it harder to get out of a chair or rise from their bed in the morning. For no apparent reason, they sometimes speak too softly to be heard. Often, their handwriting appears to have changed—their letters are smaller and cramped together.

Calm, even-tempered individuals now have unexplainable mood swings. They may become agitated or depressed. Other times their faces may seem totally blank, leaving friends and family members to guess what they are thinking or feeling. This lack of expression and facial movement in PD is known as "masked face." Many patients who display it may also remain in one position for long periods of time or move their limbs with an awkward slowness.

While the person is often aware that something is wrong, he or she may not be able to pinpoint precisely what it is. Instead, a friend or family member may first see that the person seems especially stiff or has slowed down remarkably.

Many individuals in the early stages of Parkinson's will not consult a doctor until the symptoms begin to interfere with their lifestyle. This may not happen until the tremor makes it difficult to hold a newspaper, eat a bowl of soup, or simply rest one's hands quietly on a table. Ironically, PD tremors can often be controlled while the person completes a specific task and then return with a vengeance when the task is completed and the individual begins to relax.

It's difficult to know exactly how many people have Parkinson's disease since its symptoms are often mistaken for the first signs of aging. Even those who seek medical attention may be misdiagnosed since early PD symptoms imitate those of many other medical conditions. According to the National Institute of Neurological Disorders and

Stroke—"People with Parkinson's disease may be told by their doctors that they have other disorders or, conversely, people with similar diseases may be initially diagnosed as having Parkinson's disease."[5]

In any case, Parkinson's disease is an illness that the United States cannot afford to ignore. An estimated 50,000 Americans are diagnosed with Parkinson's disease every year and more than 500,000 are affected at any one time. Estimating the actual cost of PD to our society is difficult. According to the National Parkinson Foundation, each patient spends an average of $2,500 on medications per year. With the additional expense of doctor's visits, Social Security payments, nursing-home expenditures, and lost income, the total financial cost to the nation is estimated at more than $5.6 billion per year. And, of course, the emotional cost of Parkinson's disease to individuals and their families is immeasurable.

Diagnosis

Could a person with Parkinson's disease be easily misdiagnosed? Since the classic symptoms are clearly identifiable, you might think that diagnosing PD would be a simple matter. Doctors often consider these symptoms as an important factor in their diagnosis. As one physician pointed out—"If truth be told, the diagnosis for Parkinson's disease is often obvious. Parkinsonism reduces a person's motor activity, the frequency of their facial expressions, their movement in general. Walking is slower. Less stable. The person loses balance easily. He is sometimes bent over. There really is a new and overall kind of ploddingness that was not there before."[1]

Yet the diagnosis of PD, especially in the early stages, is not simple. The physician must first eliminate several other types of parkinsonism. Also, a broad range of other symptoms that occur with PD must be considered. While these symptoms are not part of the classic Parkinson's syndrome, they are often seen in people with PD. Some symptoms are relatively minor while others are more troublesome. However, it is impossible to know which of these symptoms any particular PD patient may experience or the degree to which that person will be affected. Some of these symptoms are discussed below.

DEPRESSION

Depression, a fairly common problem, is associated with numerous medical ailments. PD patients who become depressed usually do so at the beginning of the illness. Yet if the person becomes depressed before any classic PD symptoms occur, the depression may not alert a physician to the onset of Parkinson's disease.

EMOTIONAL CHANGES

Some patients react emotionally as well as physically to PD. As the illness progresses, they feel their bodies change and their ability in some areas diminishes. A sixty-one-year-old man who had been diagnosed with Parkinson's disease the previous year described how his illness made him feel. "I've been feeling a bit more depressed lately, unable to do things that I so much enjoyed throughout the years. Sailing, tennis, skiing, have been replaced with walking and golf one to three times a week. It is fun, but it's not the same. Driving a car even seems more of a challenge. So much so, that more times than not, my wife drives me."[2]

Formerly confident individuals may grow anxious, insecure, and dependent on close friends and family members. They often avoid new challenges or situations they believe they aren't up to. Not wishing acquaintances or extended family members to know the extent of their impairment, they may avoid travel, parties, or holiday gatherings.

People with PD sometimes experience memory loss and find they are unable to think as quickly as before. But even though they may need more time to concentrate, their ability to reason is unaffected. The question of whether Parkinson's disease can ultimately cause intellectual loss or *dementia* remains controversial.

PROBLEMS WITH SWALLOWING AND CHEWING

Once Parkinson's disease has progressed somewhat, the muscles used to swallow may begin to function less effectively. This can be a problem since food and saliva then tend to collect in the patient's mouth and in the back of the throat. As a result the person may drool or in some cases even choke. Although PD is not fatal, a number of people with Parkinson's disease have choked to death due to this problem.

CHANGES IN SPEECH

About half of all people with Parkinson's find that the illness affects their speech. Some individuals speak too softly or in a monotone. Others talk too quickly, hesitate before speaking, or develop a tendency to slur or repeat themselves. Such changes can make anyone self-conscious about speaking. Some of these speech problems can be helped by working with a speech therapist.

DIFFICULTIES WITH ELIMINATION

Parkinson's disease can affect the autonomic nervous system which regulates smooth muscle activity—including the bowel and bladder muscles. The outcome varies among patients, with some finding it exceedingly difficult to urinate, while others can't control their urine and must wear adult diapers.

When the intestinal tract functions more slowly due to PD, the individual may become constipated. The problem grows worse if the person doesn't drink enough fluid, has an improper diet, and is inactive. In severe cases, people have been hospitalized for treatment, and it's essential that PD patients who become constipated seek help if the problem persists for more than a few days.

SKIN PROBLEMS

People with PD may experience changes in their skin over a period of time. Facial skin often becomes excessively oily—especially along the forehead and the nose. Patients may also develop dandruff if their scalp becomes too oily. Parkinson's disease may also cause excessive sweating.

DIFFICULTY SLEEPING

PD patients have reported a variety of sleep disorders—including restless sleep, nightmares, and exhaustion during the day. When treating sleep disorders, it is difficult for a physician to determine if the patient's problem is due to PD or the medications prescribed to treat it, or the stress of adjusting to the illness. Doctors emphasize that it's important for PD patients not to take over-the-counter drugs without their physician's knowledge. This can disrupt their sleep and may create other more serious problems.

In addition to recognizing any secondary PD symptoms, physicians must also distinguish between the many forms of parkinsonism. Some problems are common to all types of parkinsonism. Yet the various forms of the illness differ from one another as well as from *primary (or idiopathic) Parkinson's disease*—the form we have discussed so far in this book. Several other types of parkinsonism are described below.

POSTENCEPHALITIC PARKINSONISM

This extremely serious movement disorder can neurologically cripple its victims. In some cases the patient becomes catatonic—remaining in a frozen-like state—unable to talk, move about, or interact with others.

Postencephalitic parkinsonism came to the public's attention in 1918 when a viral disease known as *encephalitis lethargica* struck people around the world. Before the disease mysteriously disappeared

28

in the 1920s, nearly five million people around the globe were stricken. In the United States, where the ailment was known as "sleeping sickness," one-third of its victims died and many of the survivors developed postencephalitic parkinsonism.

In 1990, the award-winning film, *Awakenings,* portrayed the work of neurologist Oliver Sacks with postencephalitic parkinsonism patients in a New York City hospital. Using levodopa, an anti-Parkinson's drug that was then in its early experimental phase, Sacks managed to temporarily release these patients from their catatonic statue-like existence. For the first time in decades, many were able to leave the hospital on field trips to enjoy New York City and one another's company. Sadly, levodopa's effect on postencephalitic parkinsonism was not long lasting and the patients eventually reverted to their former condition.

DRUG-INDUCED PARKINSONISM

Some drugs used for psychiatric disorders, such as chlorpromazine and haloperidol, have brought on PD symptoms, especially among the elderly. A study conducted by researchers at Harvard Medical School in Boston involving 19,929 participants revealed that older people taking medication for mental or emotional problems were about twice as likely to be given anti-Parkinson's drugs by their physicians. "Because the symptoms of true Parkinson's are indistinguishable from drug-induced Parkinson's, physicians need to review the patient's medication record," stressed researcher Mark Monane.[3]

Yet anti-Parkinson's drugs are of no use at all to these patients. "[Anti-Parkinson's drugs] . . . are completely ineffective in treating drug-induced Parkinson's, while subjecting patients to the side effects of the drugs [which include hallucinations, low blood pressure, and sleep problems]," observed Jerry Avorn, the lead researcher on the Harvard study.[4] Stanley Slater, of the National Institute on Aging in Bethesda, Maryland, added—"These results should raise the question in doctors' minds of thinking of a drug-related cause for the sudden onset of Parkinson's disease."[5]

Fortunately, drug-induced parkinsonism is not permanent and can be reversed if the medication is stopped or in some cases if the dosage is sufficiently lowered. Several drugs used to treat stomach disorders, such as metoclopramide, and others prescribed for high blood pressure, like resperine, can also bring on these symptoms.

STRIATONIGRAL DEGENERATION

Unlike primary Parkinson's disease, this form of parkinsonism damages the substantia nigra only slightly but other parts of the brain are seriously affected. Individuals with striatonigral degeneration become increasingly rigid and restricted in their movements. This illness also progresses more rapidly than primary Parkinson's disease.

ARTERIOSCLEROTIC PARKINSONISM

This type of parkinsonism may appear after a number of small strokes have damaged the brain's blood vessels. While the hallmark tremor of primary Parkinson's rarely appears, the affected individual's mental abilities and life skills usually erode. The medications most commonly used to treat primary Parkinson's disease are generally of little value in treating arteriosclerotic parkinsonism.

TOXIN-INDUCED PARKINSONISM

Exposure to environmental toxins such as manganese dust, carbon disulfide, and carbon monoxide can sometimes result in toxin-induced parkinsonism. As mentioned earlier, the chemical MPTP is responsible for a form of parkinsonism that is very much like primary Parkinson's disease. Studies of the effects of MPTP on lab animals have been conducted to learn more about PD in general and develop better ways to treat it.

PARKINSONISM-DEMENTIA COMPLEX OF GUAM

This form of parkinsonism is so named because it occurs only among the Chamorro people of Guam and the Mariana Islands in the Pacific. Unlike primary Parkinson's disease, this illness is fatal and tends to progress rapidly. Most patients die within five years.

Scientists are unsure of this disease's origin, but suspect its cause may be environmental. Some researchers think the disease may be related to a type of flour the native people make from the toxic seed of the cycad plant. This flour has been a mainstay in the islanders' diet for many years. Whenever it became especially difficult for imported supplies to reach the island, such as during World War II, the flour was often used instead of rice and other staples. However, while several studies support this theory, other research has failed to show any link between the flour and parkinsonism-dementia complex of Guam.

PARKINSONISM AS A COMPANION TO OTHER ILLNESSES

At times parkinsonian symptoms go hand in hand with such neurological disorders as Shy-Drager syndrome (also known as multiple system atrophy), Huntington's disease, Alzheimer's disease, and others.

A neurologist must eliminate all other possible forms of parkinsonism before arriving at a diagnosis of primary Parkinson's, since the various forms of this illness require different courses of treatment. Unfortunately, no definitive blood or laboratory tests are available as yet to identify primary Parkinson's disease. To ensure that the patient receives the proper medication, the physician may need to observe the individual over a period of time. The doctor must also gather a complete medical and personal history from the patient. The following questions are typical.

- What has your general state of health been like?

- How quickly did your symptoms progress?
- Describe how your general health has changed over the past year. How has it changed in the past six months?

- Do you have trouble sleeping through the night?

- Describe your daily diet and exercise regimen.

- Does your home or work environment expose you to any chemicals or toxic wastes? If so, do you know which substances these are?

- Did any of your past experiences involve the use of chemicals or dyes?

- Have you ever had a particularly serious and prolonged flu during your youth?

- Do you have any chronic illnesses? If so, what are they?

Some of these questions may not seem directly related to Parkinson's disease. But the physician must have a well-rounded picture of the patient's general lifestyle and possible medical problems. Robert Barrett, a New York neurologist, described how taking a patient's medical and personal history helped him diagnose a case of Parkinson's disease—"I have a patient who developed Parkinson's disease at age sixty-five. He's a psychiatrist who lives in an old Victorian house . . . where he sees patients. This man tells me that for years people have been coming into his office and saying that they smell gas. Finally he had the gas lines checked and . . . leaks were found. . . . Was there a relationship between this man's condition and the many years he spent inhaling the gas?"[6] This proved to be the case.

A series of medical tests can also be helpful in eliminating other possible illnesses. A thorough physical exam will include blood, urine, and cholesterol measurements. If indicated, the doctor will also order an electroencephalogram (EEG) and any necessary CAT scans or X rays. Depending on the person's age and symptoms, other tests may also be prescribed.

If the patient doesn't display a particular symptom while in the physician's office, some specific diagnostic tricks may be used to bring it on. If the characteristic Parkinson's disease tremor hasn't appeared, for example, the physician may place a thin sheet of paper over the person's hands to see if the paper lies still or vibrates slightly. The individual may also be asked to draw a simple object to see if the person's hand reveals the typical unsteadiness of someone with a PD tremor. Any forms the patient has filled out, such as a medical history or insurance form, may be reviewed to see if the writing becomes smaller toward the end of the sentence.

To check for rigidity, doctors may ask patients to

simply walk across the room. They look to see if the patient shuffles or walks on tip-toe, or if the person's arms hang limply at his or her sides. Physicians also manipulate the individual's limbs during the physical exam to check for the rigidity that frequently signals Parkinson's disease. Neurologist Dr. John Dorman described the process.

"If I asked a normal person to lie down and totally relax and give me no resistance whatsoever, and if I picked his arm up, it would be floppy, like a rag doll. With Parkinson's disease, a patient's arm tends to be more stiff. If you move the joints back and forth, they never seem really to relax. Instead you feel a catching, slotted movement as you manipulate them—bup, bup, bup, like a racket. Cogwheeling. This cogwheeling is, in effect, related to the tremor."[7]

To test for bradykinesia (slow movement), the doctor evaluates how quickly an individual suspected of having PD can complete specific movements and tasks. Patients are often asked to quickly tap their thumbs and fingers together a number of times. Although the individual will be able to do so at first, it will become increasingly difficult. Patients may also be asked to tap a desk or the floor several times with their fingers or feet. If any of these movements appear jerky, slow, or irregular after the first few times, the patient may be exhibiting bradykinesia. A patient may also be timed doing a picture puzzle or completing a simple task that requires both thinking and hand-eye

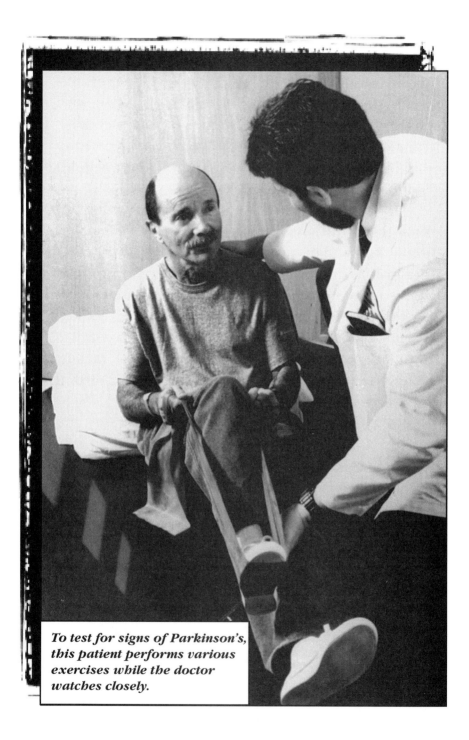

To test for signs of Parkinson's, this patient performs various exercises while the doctor watches closely.

coordination. Still another test for bradykinesia involves asking the patient to quickly rise after being seated. Many PD patients need to rock their bodies back and forth before they are able to lift themselves up.

Testing in a physician's office for impaired posture and balance can be quite revealing as well. Patients may be asked to walk back and forth or stand on one foot. The examining physician may also lightly push the patient's chest to see if the person steps back stiffly as those with PD frequently do.

Being diagnosed with Parkinson's disease can be difficult for both patients and their loved ones. They will need some time to digest the news and face how the condition will affect their future. They need to learn about the available resources and treatment options. This will be the first step on the path to coping with PD. As one man whose wife had been diagnosed with Parkinson's disease put it:

"No one is ever ready to accept Parkinson's disease or the effect of the disease on the patient or the spouse of the patient. It is, however, necessary for both to realize and accept the changes that must be made in their individual lifestyles. From my professional training as a design engineer, I have known for years that every decision is a question of trade-offs. My wife Ruth has accepted this engineering fact,

and this is how we plan our lives on a day-to-day basis. Other than consideration for other people's rights and feelings, your decisions must be based entirely on what is in your best interest. Your real friends are willing to accept any decisions that are made in this regard. . . . It has been stated that each patient must understand himself. It should also be stated that the spouse of each patient must also completely understand the patient. This understanding does not come easily, but must be cultivated and fine-tuned. . . . As long as life goes on, one must assume that some breaks will come, so we continue to smile at each sunrise."[8]

CHAPTER 3

Treatment

Parkinson's disease can be an especially difficult illness to cope with. At this time, no cure or medication effectively halts the disease's advance. Therefore, to treat PD, doctors generally use drugs that will lessen their patients' symptoms with the least number of side effects. Many physicians devise a conservative treatment plan for their PD patients. A diagnosis of PD doesn't necessarily mean that the person will immediately start medication. Instead, a doctor may wait until the symptoms interfere with the individual's daily functioning before prescribing drugs.

How a PD symptom handicaps an individual depends on the individual's particular tasks or duties. A hand tremor is far more troublesome to a surgeon than to a retired schoolteacher. But a disability cannot be judged solely in terms of job performance. If PD symptoms prohibit someone from engaging in a favorite sport or hobby, that person may wish to go on medication. In any case, the decision to initiate drug treatment is best left between the patient and doctor. However, before starting any medication, it is important that the patient and the patient's family know what to expect. Patients who expect to regain their former state of health are likely to be disappointed. Medications generally used to treat Parkinson's disease include the following:

LEVODOPA
Levodopa, also known as L-dopa, is presently the drug that best combats many of the symptoms of Parkinson's disease. It's actually a simple chemical found naturally in plants and animals. However, when manufactured as a drug, levodopa crosses from the intestinal tract to the blood and eventually reaches the brain. Nerve cells there use levodopa to manufacture dopamine—the neurotransmitter that is deficient in PD. By restoring most of the patient's dopamine, many PD symptoms may be sharply reduced.

Doctors can't give their patients actual dopamine as this chemical cannot cross the blood-brain barrier—an intricate webbing of small blood vessels and cells that filters the blood reaching the brain. The introduction of levodopa in the 1960s was an important breakthrough in treating Parkinson's. By delaying the start of extremely debilitating symp-

PD patients may turn to medical drugs in order to keep doing an interesting hobby or playing a favorite sport.

toms in some patients, the drug enhanced their productivity and quality of life for a number of years.

Shortly after beginning treatment with levodopa, PD patients often improve dramatically. Some may even feel cured, but it's important to remember that there is no cure. The drug makes the symptoms subside, but it cannot restore cells or retard the disease's progression.

While levodopa's value should not be underestimated, it has some drawbacks. Levodopa is effective for only about three-quarters of all patients with PD. In addition, it does not lessen all the symptoms equally. Often the major benefit is a sharp reduction in bradykinesia and rigidity. Tremors tend to improve, too, but a patient's impaired balance and other symptoms remain unaffected in most cases.

Like almost every medication used to treat Parkinson's disease, levodopa may produce some unpleasant side effects. These can include nausea, vomiting, low blood pressure, restlessness—and in some unusual instances—confusion. While taking levodopa, PD patients may also experience some involuntary movement of their limbs or other body parts. Known as *dyskinesia,* this can take the form of nodding, twitching, or jerking. Dyskinesia can be mild or severe and the uncontrollable movements may be either rapid or slow.

Dyskinesia usually occurs in individuals who have taken large amounts of levodopa over a long period of time. This side effect can only be lessened by lowering the amount of levodopa prescribed or by taking drugs that block the dopamine's action. The latter may not be a desirable choice since the symptoms for which levodopa was originally prescribed may then reappear. Ideally, the doctor and patient will work closely together to find the right balance between the drug's effectiveness and its negative side effects.

Yet even when those side effects are tolerable, patients may have other problems taking levodopa for a prolonged period. Some experience what is known as the "wearing-off effect." This occurs when the patients' symptoms worsen before they take their first pill of the day as well as when each dose of the medication begins to wear off. As a result, patients feel the drug's maximum effectiveness for a significantly shorter time each day.

The "on-off effect" is still another problem some people taking levodopa must deal with. With the on-off effect, PD patients experience sudden unpredictable changes in their ability to move their limbs easily. They may be functioning normally when, without warning, their movements take on the slowness and rigidity characteristic of Parkinson's. These changes, which are entirely out of the patient's control, may occur several times throughout the day. The on-off effect usually indicates that the body's reaction to the drug has changed or that the disease has progressed to the point at which the medication is no longer as effective.

Physicians may take different approaches to handling the wearing-off effect and the on-off effect.

Some doctors find that their patients are helped by taking levodopa more frequently in smaller amounts. Others attempt to improve their patients' response by taking them off levodopa for a few days before having them go back on the medication. This method, known as a "drug holiday," should never be tried without a doctor's supervision. Withdrawing from the medication too rapidly can result in severe health consequences.

LEVODOPA/CARBIDOPA (SINEMET)

Levodopa is most commonly prescribed with the drug carbidopa—under the trade name Sinemet. This combination helps eliminate some of the side effects caused by taking levodopa alone. The combined drug tends to reduce the nausea and vomiting common to many individuals who take only levodopa. It also sends more levodopa directly to the brain by blocking its conversion to dopamine in the large intestine and blood. Patients taking Sinemet require smaller levodopa doses and often avoid the side effects associated with large doses over an extended period. Sinemet comes in two forms—regular, which is quickly absorbed by the body, and timed-release, which is absorbed over several hours. Patients experiencing the wearing-off effect of levodopa frequently find it helpful to use the timed-release capsules.

SELEGILINE

Selegiline is often the first drug given to people diagnosed with PD. It is effective in about sixty

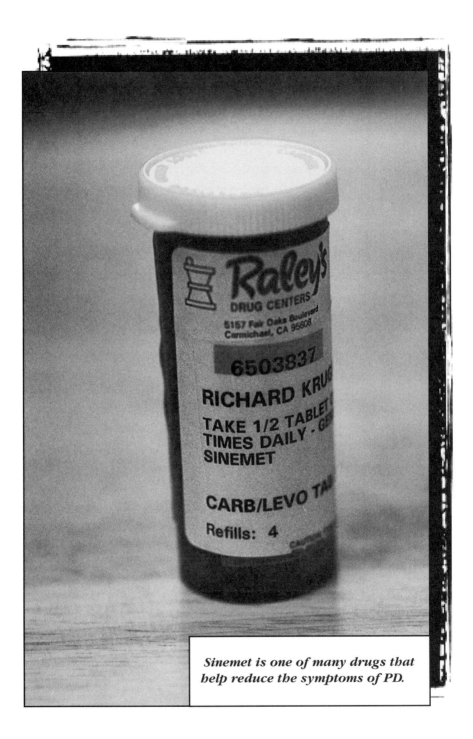

Sinemet is one of many drugs that help reduce the symptoms of PD.

percent of cases and is usually taken for about a year before the disease's progression demands levodopa. Selegiline, also known as Deprenyl and Eldepryl, interrupts the enzyme that destroys dopamine—thereby delaying the breakdown of natural dopamine as well as of the dopamine formed with levodopa.

Some patients have trouble sleeping while on selegiline, so this drug is usually taken early in the morning. At times, selegiline is given to patients with more advanced PD who are also taking levodopa. In these cases, it may lessen levodopa's wearing-off effect. However, the drawback is that selegiline may also either worsen or bring on dyskinesia in the patient.

A number of animal studies have shown that selegiline protects dopamine-producing cells from the toxic effects of the chemical MPTP. Researchers are continuing to study this drug to determine its full potential use for humans.

BROMOCRIPTINE AND PERGOLIDE

Also known as dopamine receptor agonists, these drugs imitate dopamine's action on the brain. At times they are prescribed in the early stage of PD, although neither is as effective as levodopa in lessening rigidity and bradykinesia. Bromocriptine and pergolide may also be used in the later stages of PD along with levodopa to reduce the wearing-off and on-off effects of the drug. Some PD patients taking bromocriptine and pergolide experience side effects such as hallucinations, confusion, dyskinesia, nightmares, nausea, and vomiting.

ANTICHOLINERGIC DRUGS

Before levodopa was developed, anticholinergic drugs were most commonly prescribed for PD patients. These include trihexyphenidyl (Artane), benztropine (Cogentin), and biperiden (Akineton). While some drugs used to combat PD affect dopamine levels in the brain, anticholinergics serve a different purpose. They suppress the action of another substance in the brain as acetylcholine becomes more pronounced when dopamine levels drop.

Anticholinergics are not always helpful—only about half of PD patients exhibit some temporary improvement on these drugs. When they do work, these drugs tend to reduce the patient's tremor and rigidity. Anticholinergics have sometimes proved beneficial when taken along with levodopa or bromocriptine. Common side effects of anticholinergics include dry mouth, constipation, hallucinations, memory loss, blurred vision, and confusion.

AMANTADINE

Amantadine, also known as Symmetrel, is a drug that may be used early in the course of PD to reduce some of the symptoms. Amantadine may also be taken with levodopa or another anti-Parkinson's drug. Often, amantadine's effectiveness decreases after a few months and at that point patients may be taken off it. If these individuals go back on the medication at a later date, they may find it somewhat beneficial again. Amantadine's side effects can include skin problems, fuzzy vision, and depression.

MIRAPEX (PRAMIPEXOLE DIHYDROCHLORIDE)

Approved by the U.S. Food and Drug Administration in July 1997, Mirapex is the newest drug available for the treatment of Parkinson's disease. Like many other anti-Parkinson medications, it can be used alone in the early stages of PD or taken in conjunction with levodopa when the illness has advanced. Mirapex is believed to work by stimulating dopamine receptors in the brain to enhance the patient's movements. Among Mirapex's most common side effects are insomnia, dizziness, hallucinations, and nausea.

All the medications currently prescribed for Parkinson's disease only relieve or reduce some of the symptoms in an attempt to make the patient more comfortable. Researchers continue to try to find a more effective drug with fewer side effects.

However, a recent advance for Parkinson's disease patients that does not involve drugs is a brain implant that helps control tremors. Approved in August 1997 by the Food and Drug Administration, this pacemaker type of device is surgically implanted in the brain and sends out tiny electrical shocks that block or override the brain signals causing the tremor.

Patients can program the device themselves through an external unit and turn it on or off by running a magnet over their chest. The operation to install this device takes five hours and costs about $25,000. While this implant has no effect on other PD symptoms, it allows some people with severe tremors to once again cut up their own food, dress themselves, and sign their name.

The National Institute of Neurological Disorders and Stroke (NINDS) has been a world leader in research on various neurological disorders including Parkinson's disease. In addition to conducting a wide range of basic laboratory studies and clinical trials at its own location, the NINDS also sponsors research at various institutions throughout the world. Their efforts include studies on how the disease progresses as well as new treatment options.

The NINDS and the National Institute of Mental Health also jointly support two national brain specimen banks for research purposes. To help scientists better study and understand the disease, people with PD specify that following their death their brain tissue be donated to these banks or other privately run brain-bank centers.

Among the particularly interesting research projects currently underway are studies involving a naturally occurring protein known as glial-cell-line-derived neurotrophic factor (GDNF). Preliminary studies indicate that GDNF may actually protect, nourish, and restore nerve cells destroyed by Parkinson's disease. One early report published by a Colorado-based research team in 1993, described GDNF's beneficial effect on brain neurons damaged by Parkinson's disease. Later on, the work of Lars Olson and his colleagues at the Karolinska Institute in Stockholm, Sweden, confirmed these findings.

Olson had injected mice with GDNF before administering a dose of the compound MPTP (a cause of drug-induced Parkinson's disease). The results showed that the GDNF saved approximately half of the dopamine-producing neurons that would have normally died under these circumstances. Further findings also showed that GDNF may be able to repair and restore dopamine-producing neurons damaged by PD. This process was revealed when the research team gave the toxic MPTP compound to a group of lab mice and about two weeks later injected GDNF directly into the rodents' brains. At that point, the surviving dopamine-producing neurons began sending out additional fibers. Within a week, the researchers observed an improvement in the brain's supply of dopamine.

The Swedish researchers' results were confirmed by another study conducted in San Francisco, California. There, Dr. Klaus D. Beck and his associates cut the fiber-like extensions of the dopamine-producing neurons in a group of lab rats. The researchers expected about fifty percent of the cut neurons to die. But when Beck's team administered GDNF to the rats' brains immediately after the cuts, only about fifteen percent of the dopamine-producing neurons were destroyed.

Similar promising results have been reported elsewhere in the United States. Neurobiologist Don M. Gash of the University of Kentucky College of Medicine and his colleagues gave MPTP to a group of rhesus monkeys and, as expected, the animals exhibited Parkinson's disease symptoms. However, every month, the researchers injected GDNF into the affected regions of these lab animals' brains.

After the GDNF treatments, the monkeys exhibited a significant improvement in posture and balance and were considerably less rigid. The animals maintained their improvement as long as their monthly dose of GDNF continued. As the monkeys' brains revealed increased concentrations of dopamine in the substantia nigra, Gash and his colleagues suspect that GDNF may benefit the patient by better regulating the dopamine in that part of the brain. Research like this brings the scientific world one step closer to solving the mysteries of Parkinson's.

Meanwhile, in addition to drug therapy, people with Parkinson's disease can presently take other measures to relieve their symptoms and improve their lives. Although no specific diet is recommended for PD patients, well-balanced nutritious meals are advisable for everyone and can be especially important for those with the illness. At one time it was thought that a form of vitamin E known as tocopherol might delay PD symptoms, but this has been disproved. However, if an individual with PD is taking the drug levodopa, a high-protein diet might limit the medication's effectiveness.

Unfortunately, people with PD may be prone to malnutrition. This is especially true when difficult swallowing and slowed movement make preparing and eating food difficult and time-consuming. Involuntary movements as well as hand tremors can also make mealtimes discouraging. Also, many drugs commonly taken for Parkinson's disease cause nausea, vomiting, and decreased appetite and aggravate the situation.

It is important to keep these risk factors in mind when helping patients with PD plan their menus. If a person with PD experiences a weight loss of more than ten percent of body weight in less than a few months, that individual may not be getting all the necessary nutrients for good health. In such cases, the patient may need to work with a dietician who can balance the individual's medical concerns with a sound nutritional program.

Many people with Parkinson's disease also find exercise extremely helpful in improving their mobility. Doctors often suggest physical therapy or special muscle-strengthening exercises to loosen their patients' rigid muscles and relieve tension. While no form of exercise can stop or delay Parkinson's disease, the person may be less disabled as the illness progresses.

The American Parkinson's Disease Association suggests the following exercise tips for those with Parkinson's disease:

- Choose a time to exercise when you are well rested and moving most freely.

- Wear loose, comfortable clothing and shoes with good support.

- Structure your program to include adequate rest periods, or divide your program into several shorter sessions.

Many PD patients increase their mobility through regular exercise.

• Move slowly through each exercise. Avoid "bouncing" motions.

• Maintain normal breathing throughout exercises.[1]

Specialized exercises can help those with balance or walking problems, as well as help individuals improve their speech or swallowing. Some patients feel that exercise boosts their spirits and helps them keep a positive attitude. While numerous people with PD do exercises that target specific parts of their bodies, any type of physical activity including walking, gardening, or swimming may prove beneficial.

Even virtual reality may soon play a role in improving the mobility of people with Parkinson's. While working with a group of PD patients, researchers at the University of Washington found that these individuals walked more easily when they were following a trail of coins, cards, buttons, or similar objects placed on the floor at intervals equaling an average stride. Such occurrences are known as kinesia paradox—the eye tricks the mind to enhance the neural transmission lines between the brain and the legs so that the person's movement is less hesitant.

Using virtual reality with Parkinson's disease patients would allow the same flow of movement without having to actually lay out the trail of objects. The University of Washington researchers achieved this by using a pair of specially made virtual-reality glasses that cast a similar path for the patient to follow.

When wearing these glasses, the person sees videotaped visual cues such as a line of moving balls. The videotape repeats the same image so the person can walk smoothly. This device eliminates the need for the bulky headsets and goggles generally used for virtual-reality images. Although more work needs to be done on this concept, such devices might eventually be an important mobility aid for people with Parkinson's.

CHAPTER 4

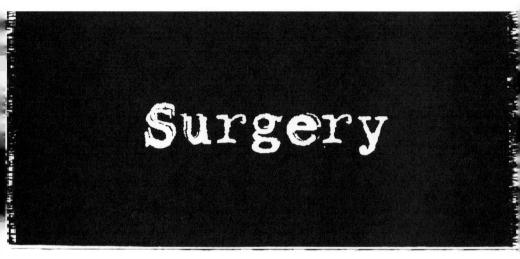

Surgery

Besides relying on a healthy lifestyle and anti-Parkinson's drugs to combat PD—surgery is another option. Before the use of levodopa, doctors often resorted to surgery in treating severe cases of Parkinson's. In recent times, some of these procedures have been refined and revived. All present-day surgery to reduce PD symptoms is done stereotactically. In these operations, surgeons use a computerized system to precisely target brain cells. Then, using a needle inserted through a small hole in the skull, the surgeons either destroy or electrically stimulate the pinpointed cell group. Operations performed on people who have Parkinson's disease include the following:

THALAMOTOMY

During this procedure, the metal tip of a probe is inserted into the thalamus (a relay station deep within the brain) to demolish the cells in this area responsible for tremors. When effective, this surgery largely eliminates the characteristic PD tremor on the opposite side of the body from which the operation is performed.

PALLIDOTOMY

In this operation, first developed in the 1950s, a group of cells is destroyed in the internal globus pallidus—a brain region from which information is transported. Several studies show that pallidotomy may improve such PD symptoms as tremors, dyskinesia, rigidity, and bradykinesia. Researchers suspect that the operation's success results from interrupting the neural pathways between the globus pallidus and other brain regions.

PALLIDAL OR THALAMIC STIMULATION

This procedure targets the same areas of the brain as the two surgeries previously described. But here the brain cells are stimulated electrically to halt their functioning, rather than being destroyed. Some surgeons prefer this procedure because the brain change is not permanent. But like other operations, much more needs to be learned about the procedure. Presently, these surgeries are performed only on individuals with severe cases of Parkinson's disease for whom drug therapy has been ineffective.

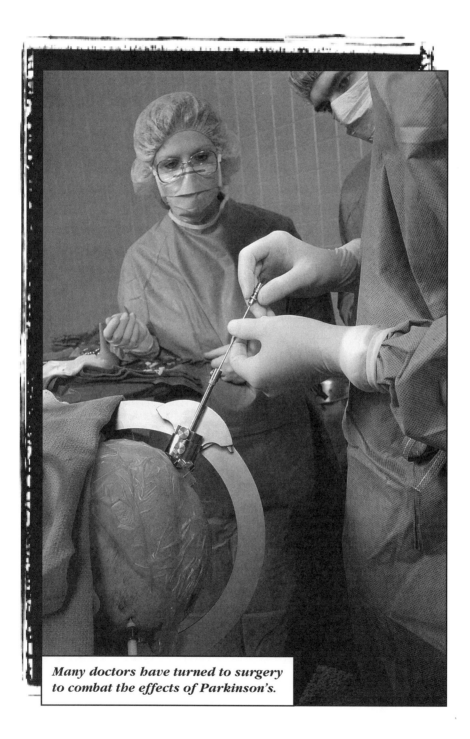

Many doctors have turned to surgery to combat the effects of Parkinson's.

Perhaps the procedure that best captured the media's limelight in recent times is pallidotomy. A 1995 segment of the TV news program *Prime Time Live* featured a middle-aged man with PD whose tremors had progressed to the point where he could no longer hold his coffee mug. He agreed to have a pallidotomy. Viewers watched as a strategically placed surgical probe destroyed a pea-sized piece of his brain and allowed him to regain control of his body for the first time in years.

Since that episode aired, numerous other medical and news programs, including *60 Minutes*, have cited instances of remarkable outcomes brought about by this surgical option. Parkinson's disease patients and their families began to think that this 1950s procedure might be the answer they'd been hoping for. Neurosurgeons across the country wanted to know more about the operation.

But the television and magazine success stories did not show the whole picture. Important questions needed to be answered. How often and to what extent did people with Parkinson's disease actually reap the highly publicized benefits of pallidotomy? Was the medical community aware of all the procedure's short- and long-term risks?

Some of the lavish praise for pallidotomies came from Swedish neurosurgeon Lauri Laitinen, who had continued performing pallidotomies on PD patients after most doctors abandoned surgery in favor of drug therapy. However, Laitinen had tested and refined the procedure somewhat in order to improve the results. Surgeons performing this operation in the 1950s just made nicks in various parts of the brain involved with movement, but Laitinen zeroed in on a particular part of the globus pallidus.

In 1992, Laitinen and his associates published their results. They reported that 35 of their first 38 patients experienced "complete or almost complete relief of rigidity" while 30 of the 38 had "excellent or good long-lasting tremor relief."[1]

However, when other surgeons tried to achieve such results, it became clear that there was a lot more to learn. For a few weeks following the operations, patients often seemed dramatically improved, but these outcomes did not always last. And it proved difficult for doctors to determine precisely where to insert their surgical probe to improve the more subtle PD symptoms, such as rigidity and slowness. Accurately evaluating the results of a pallidotomy could be challenging as well since it was sometimes hard to distinguish encouraging post-operative results from the symptom fluctuations that normally occur in Parkinson's.

Nevertheless, as more of these surgeries were performed, some valuable information was amassed. Laszlo Tamas, a neurosurgeon at Parkinson's Institute in Sunnyvale, California, performed a number of pallidotomies and found the surgery to be most helpful in reducing dyskinesia and rigidity. A surgical team at New York University learned that younger patients tended to benefit most from pallidotomies while people who had never responded to L-dopa did not improve with surgery. These doctors also found that the small group of PD patients with dementia (irrational thinking) were worse after the surgery.

The procedure also involves risks that are frequently underemphasized. Although all brain surgery carries the possibility of stroke, in a pallidotomy a number of other concerns arise as well. When removing a brain tumor, the surgeon has the clearly marked boundaries of the growth for guidance, but the area targeted in a pallidotomy is extremely small and looks exactly like the surrounding tissue. An error of only three millimeters not only renders the surgery useless but can diminish the patient's vision or even cause paralysis. According to neurosurgeon Patrick J. Kelly who has performed pallidotomies at New York University Medical Center—"Even relative to other sorts of brain surgery, there's not much margin for error here. It's an art, and training is critical."[2]

Yet despite the risks and the varied outcomes, many people with Parkinson's disease clamor for the surgery. The current demand exists though some doctors have told their patients that in five years or so, the operation will probably be significantly improved. Of course, this means little to patients who are likely to be too ill and debilitated by then to qualify for the procedure.

Meanwhile, doctors have already taken steps to upgrade the surgery. One type of enhanced pallidotomy requires doctors to work closely with a neurophysiologist during the operation. The neurophysiologist listens carefully to the electrical activity in various parts of the brain. The overactive brain cells to be targeted give off a distinctly recognizable sound allowing the surgical team to easily and accurately pinpoint them. In the future, such precise information on brain physiology will help standardize the surgery's basic techniques, allowing doctors to know exactly where and how large to make the hole.

Whether or not patients consider their pallidotomies successful often depends on their options and viewpoint. One fifty-five-year old California engineer who had a pallidotomy feels that his surgery was worth it despite the fact that following his initial improvement he had to resume his medication and deal with some recurring symptoms. Nevertheless, he quickly points out that his face is more expressive, he sleeps better, and driving a car is no longer as much of a challenge. His medication is also more effective and he no longer fears that it will wear off, leaving him to "freeze up" in public. In describing his pallidotomy, he noted—"This is never a cure, I still have Parkinson's. But for me, and for many other people, it comes down to independence. Anything that I can do now for myself makes a big difference in my quality of life."[3]

A sixty-two-year-old woman from Birmingham, Alabama, with Parkinson's disease felt similarly about the operation. If there was a chance to improve, she was willing to try it and had announced just prior to her surgery—"The good Lord's given me the faith to fight."[4]

As her PD had progressed through the years, she found her mobility and quality of life diminished to the extent that she could not safely hold her baby granddaughter in her arms. At first she had taken the drug Sinemet, which initially reversed her symptoms. But like most anti-Parkinson drugs, it's effectiveness decreased after prolonged use, leaving her in a difficult position.

Hoping to still make the most of her life, the woman decided to have a pallidotomy. In the days following the surgery, the results looked promising. "I used to not eat sometimes when I went out with my friends because I was so embarrassed," she remarked. "Now I can sit at the table like a normal person and bring the food smoothly to my mouth." Although it's not known how long these and other positive changes will last, the woman is still glad she had the surgery. As she put it, "I'd settle for anything I can get."[5]

Another exciting surgical alternative on the horizon for people with Parkinson's disease is fetal tissue transplants. In this procedure, dopamine-producing brain cells taken from aborted fetuses are implanted into the brains of PD patients. The fetal tissue is grafted into the striatum—the area of the brain deprived of dopamine. Ideally, as the newly grafted cells grow and become an integral part of the brain, the depleted dopamine will be restored and the patient's PD symptoms will significantly decrease.

Early fetal transplant experimentation was conducted at a few centers in the United States as well as in France, England, and Sweden during the mid-1980s. About two hundred of these surgeries had been performed worldwide when a heated controversy arose over the morality of using aborted fetuses as the source of the transplanted tissue. Those who believe that life begins at conception argued that babies would be conceived and killed just to provide an ongoing supply of this highly demanded commodity.

The issue was reviewed by a medical advisory committee from the National Institute of Health which determined that the procedure was not unethical and held out hope for the future. Yet despite these findings, all federal funding for this research was banned during the administrations of President Reagan and President Bush. Unfortunately, the surgery had turned into a political rather than a medical issue. Those who favored the procedure stressed that the majority of Reagan and Bush supporters were pro-lifers who were adamantly opposed to abortion. When President Bill Clinton entered the White House in 1993 the ban was lifted by executive order.

Now U.S. scientists were free to perform fetal cell transplants, but since research in this area had been cut off so soon, they weren't certain how effective these transplants actually were. "The moratorium

The emotional debate over abortion has led many people to criticize new research that uses transplanted fetal cells in PD patients.

distorted the scientific discussion," noted D. Eugene Redmond, the leader of a Yale University transplant team. "To muster the political power to overturn it, the actual scientific accomplishments were somewhat exaggerated." His feelings were echoed by National Institutes of Health researcher William Freed who'd commented—"People thought, 'Well, it's banned, it must be something really great.'"[6]

Yet some of patients who had the transplants experienced promising results. Researchers were encouraged by a report by neurosurgeon Jeffrey H. Kordower of the Rush-Presbyterian-St. Luke's Medical Center in Chicago and his colleagues on how they had implanted fetal cells into the brain of a fifty-nine-year-old man with advanced PD. Following the transplant, the patient experienced a notable improvement in his symptoms. "He still has Parkinson's disease," Kordower observed, "but many of his problems had completely dissipated."[7] Although the patient died eighteen months later of unrelated causes, his autopsy revealed that "the fetal cells had survived in large numbers."

Some of the other surgical patients also enjoyed positive results. These patients did extremely well on standardized movement and coordination measurements. They were also able to perform the simple everyday tasks that PD had interrupted. Tying their shoes, driving a car, brushing their teeth, and combing their hair were no longer daily obstacles. And most were able to cut their medication in half.

One patient who had nearly lost his ability to

speak had avoided his old friends out of embarass-
ment. Besides being barely audible, he had become
unable to feed himself properly. He felt a great bur-
den had been lifted from him following his
transplant. Once again he spoke and ate normally
and could look forward to get-togethers with those
close to him. A year after the surgery, he gave a
Thanksgiving Day dinner party for twelve guests.
Additional enthusiastic reports included one man
who, prior to having Parkinson's disease, had been
quite athletic and could now resume hiking and
swimming. Noting these developments, one of the
participating neurosurgeons wrote, "About a third of
the patients [who'd had the transplants] have had
their lives revolutionized."[8]

If these results sound too good to be true, it's because they are. As with the early pallidotomy
results—there was more to the story. In the final
analysis, the major drawback of the fetal tissue transplants was that the outcome was highly variable
among the patients. While some improved dramatically, others derived only moderate benefits and
some achieved no long-term gains at all. Yet, as it
turned out, these patients were not the worst off. In
a few cases the patient's condition significantly dete-
riorated following the transplant.

Critics of the procedure stress that, besides the
highly variable outcomes, there were several inher-
ent dangers in the surgery itself. Although the odds
of a needle accidentally striking an artery or a crucial part of the brain are small, a few such accidents

have occurred. One patient was a fifty-five-year-old male who had suffered from PD for eight years. As a result of the error, he had a fatal stroke and subsequently died. "We knew this was an odds game," his surgeon said afterward. "Passing needles into the brain carries risk, and the risk of stroke is about 1 in 500 needle passes. At the time we'd be doing 14 to 16 needle passes on each patient. With each operation there was about a three percent chance of stroke."[9]

Skeptics further argue that the enthusiasm surrounding fetal tissue transplants is likely to fade as did an experimental surgery for Parkinson's disease in the 1980s. In that operation, dopamine-producing cells from a patient's own adrenal glands were transplanted into the individual's brain. Following Mexican neurosurgeon Ignacio Madrozo's claims of success with this procedure, hundreds of the operations were done—including about one hundred in the United States. Results showed that forty percent of the patients enjoyed beneficial effects but regressed to their former states in less than a year. Some researchers felt that adrenal gland cells would never work since they manufacture very little dopamine. "They're just not the right kind of cell," one neurosurgeon explained. "Also," he added, "they don't survive well in the brain because they don't belong there. The tissue around them doesn't provide a supportive environment."[10] Besides dealing with the lack of significant long-term improvement, these patients were also vulnerable to the standard side effects of any surgical procedure involving the brain, including respiratory problems, pneumonia, urinary tract infections, sleeplessness, confusion, heart attack, hallucination, and stroke.

So far, the ultimate outcome for fetal cell transplants appears more encouraging. But even ardent supporters of the procedure stress that there is still much more to learn. Some doctors performing the operation have expressed concern over the possible role of psychological factors in a patient's temporary improvement. Could wish fulfillment and perhaps the mystique surrounding fetal cell use play a part in these outcomes? In drug studies involving PD patients, a significant number of participants who were given a placebo (sugar pill), but believed they were taking the actual drug, reported some improvement. Could the brief improvement they experienced be similar to the short-term gains of some of the recipients of fetal cell transplants?

In an effort to answer this question and others, a number of neurosurgeons are embarking on some highly controversial studies. Half of a group of PD patients will be given actual fetal cell transplants while the other half of the study group will undergo sham operations. None of the patients will know who is having the genuine transplants as the preparation procedure will be the same for both. "The pacing and atmosphere will be nearly identical to the true tissue implant," a researcher explained in describing how the false operation will proceed. "The strategy is to do things exactly the same way, maybe even have some tissue set up in a dish, so there's time involved in picking up the tissue. We'll drill holes in the skull, the needle will be inserted into the . . . apparatus, all the calculations will be done, the timing will be exactly the same, but the needles will not drop the last centimeters into the brain."[11]

Following the surgery all study participants (those who had the actual transplant as well as those who did not) will be evaluated on their speed and precision in completing specific tasks. Their overall movement patterns will be videotaped. Everyone involved will also undergo PET scans (position-emission tomography) to enable researchers to see how well the tissue has survived and grown.

Those who undergo the sham operation will be guaranteed a chance to have an actual transplant if the study indicates that fetal cell transplants can provide long-term benefits. "We've promised them treatment, one of the participating researchers noted. "But if it's a bust, they're better off having the sham surgery rather than the real operation."[12]

The National Institutes of Health (NIH), which provided the funding for the research, will oversee the work. A special Data Safety Monitoring Committee will be able to stop the procedures if unanticipated risks or complications ensue. As C. Warren Olanow, a neurologist on the NIH's committee to oversee some of the research, explained the need for such studies—"What you don't want to do—especially with something as dramatic and publicized as fetal tissue transplantation—is put yourself in a position where you're not sure that what you're seeing is real. Is it better to expose a small number of patients to a placebo than to forego a control group and potentially expose hundreds of thousands to a procedure that may not work?"[13]

Yet while some neurosurgeons believe this research is crucial, others think that we don't know enough about the procedure to undertake this type of study. They feel the risk to those who undergo the surgery without getting the transplant is too great. "There's a 1 in 100 chance that performing craniotomies on the surgical controls could result in the formation of blood clots. If one of those patients dies, it could set the field back several years," commented neuroscientist John Sladek of the Chicago Medical School.[14]

Though the NIH's fetal transplant research continues, it's doubtful that similar projects will begin until a number of questions regarding the surgical techniques used in these operations are resolved. Presently, neurosurgeons still have different opinions regarding the precise placements of implants, the amount of fetal tissue necessary, and whether the tissue should be kept in a culture or frozen and later thawed for the transplant procedure. The debate as to whether patients receiving fetal cell transplants should be given the same immunosuppressant drugs (to prevent cell rejection) used for organ transplants continues as well.

Surgeons are also working to achieve an improved survival rate for the transplanted fetal material. Some autopsies of patients who'd had the transplant indicate that a large number of cells survived and formed connective tissue to other parts of the brain, but those results are not typical. Other autopsies, as well as animal lab tests, show that many transplanted fetal cells fail to thrive. "Although even a few surviving transplanted cells may be enough to provide clinical effects [some observable improvement], poor survival may account for variability in the results we've seen so far," a neurosurgeon involved in fetal transplant surgery noted. "People doing kidney transplants were able to get better results simply by improving their surgical techniques and their handling of the organ."[15]

Still another major obstacle is the overall lack of available fetal tissue for transplants. Researchers still do not agree on how much fetal tissue is necessary for each operation, but estimates range from one to nine fetuses. It has also been exceedingly difficult to extract any significant amount of dopamine-producing tissue from a fetus that has been damaged in an abortion.

Although these problems still cloud the issue of fetal cell transplants, researchers are actively exploring new ways to overcome such obstacles. While hoping to avoid the 1980s failure that resulted from transplanting dopamine-producing cells from the patient's own adrenal glands, scientists have searched for new ways in which a person's own body might serve as a source of transplant material. Now they hope to try cells from the patient's skin and muscle, which will be genetically engineered to produce a chemical that causes the brain to manufacture dopamine. "From a skin biopsy the size of a quarter we can produce as much tissue in two weeks as you can harvest from a hundred fetuses," said a researcher from a California biotechnology company.[16]

Scientists have looked into other possible alternatives as well, including xenotransplantation —transplanting cells from other species. These doctors have harvested tissue from fetal pigs and inserted the material into the brains of PD patients. They chose the dopamine-producing cells from a pig because these were similar to the human cells— and far more readily available.

Such experimental surgery began in April 1995 in the first FDA-approved experiment of its kind at the Lahey Hitchcock Clinic in Burlington, Massachusetts. The following October at a conference on xenotransplantation, the researchers reported that the preliminary results were encouraging. At that time, the three individuals who underwent the procedure had not rejected the transplanted fetal pig cells.

A PET scan performed on the first patient indicated that new living dopamine-producing cells were present and it was also later shown that two of the three patients had demonstrated some improvement. "Although the clinical data is preliminary, it looks promising," noted one of the participating neurosurgeons at the Third International Conference for Xenotransplantation.[17]

Since these beginning trials, fetal pig cells have been implanted in other patients. However, in these cases, the patients were not given the immunosuppressive drugs that leave an individual without protection from various infections and cancer. Instead, the fetal pig cells were treated with antibody fragments prior to being implanted. Ideally, the antibody fragments would disguise the pig protein on the surface of the fetal cells thereby preventing the body from rejecting the material. The work was termed "a bold move" by Saul R. Sanberg of the University of South Florida in Tampa and President of the American Society for Neural Transplantation.[18] However, scientists need to know much more about this process.

Further experimentation is also being conducted to test implanting dopamine-producing cells in plastic capsules. Hopefully, the dopamine would flow from the capsule while the plastic outer shell shielded the body from the foreign material, stopping the patient's immune-suppression system from rejecting it. If such a delivery system is perfected, both unmatched adult tissue and some types of animal tissue might be used—thereby ending the present supply problem.

Yet there is some new research to indicate that patients with Parkinson's disease might need more than just dopamine. Studies on completed fetal cell transplants show that in addition to dopamine, fetal cells also produce chemicals that cause nerve cells to grow. In NIH lab-animal experiments, fetal cells that did not produce dopamine, but were rich in such growth factors, were transplanted into monkeys and rats that had PD-like symptoms. The results showed that in some cases the animals's symptoms improved for up to a year.

This led scientists to wonder if the "dual effect" of dopamine and such growth-stimulating chemicals might together be responsible for the improvement in PD patients sometimes seen after fetal cell transplants. Therefore, doctors performing fetal cell transplants in the future may want to inject additional growth factors into the implanted tissue or try using just the growth-stimulating chemicals on their patients.

Nevertheless, as our present-day medical knowledge grows, so does the controversy surrounding fetal cell transplants. In various countries throughout the world, researchers, ethicists, and government policymakers have debated the ramifications of the possible routine use of fetal cell material. One such symposium organized by the Network of European CNS Transplantation and Restoration (NECTAR) groups from Munich and Hanover was held in Germany in the early 1990s. While numerous philosophical, ethical, theological, legal, and economic questions were raised, the discussion largely centered on two specific issues. The first was a not-often-mentioned but possibly important question: Can neurotransplantation (implanting one person's brain tissue into another's brain) possibly affect the recipient's personality? At one time the answer from the scientific community would have been a definite no. But more recently a number of organ transplant recipients have spoken out on this topic, leading some researchers to rethink the matter.

Could such a thing as "cell memory" possibly exist? One woman who had a heart transplant never particularly liked fried chicken but felt a strong urge for it upon her release from the hospital. She immediately went out to buy some fried chicken, which she ate with gusto and thoroughly enjoyed. When this inexplicable craving continually returned the woman gave in to it, although she admitted that it seemed strange to her. Some time later she learned that her organ donor had been a young man whose favorite food was fried chicken.

There have been numerous similar stories. Organ transplant recipients have felt uncannily at home in places they've never been, have had strange dreams, or changes in taste that they subsequently learned were characteristic of their donor's personality. Are all these coincidences related in some way to their transplants? If so, could cells placed directly in someone's brain magnify this phenomenon even further? The researchers concluded that there is a difference between transplanting intact pieces of fetal central nervous tissue and just injecting suspended fetal cells. The cell option was favored since whole pieces of neuronal (brain) tissue could contain independent neuronal networks or possible parts of a separate personality. In any case, further investigation will be needed to help clear up these concerns.

The other issue dominating the symposium in Germany was the ethical concerns prompted by the use of fetal cells in transplants. Could the scarcity of fetal material eventually lead to abuses? Might a wealthy person pay a woman to conceive a child and purposely abort it to gain usable fetal tissue? The "slippery slope" factor was also discussed at the meeting. According to this reasoning the therapeutic use of fetal cells for medical purposes might ultimately sway some women's attitudes toward abortion—eventually resulting in more abortions being performed.

Although viewpoints on the ethics of using aborted fetuses for transplantation differed, everyone agreed that further discussion on the issue was crucial. Perhaps strict guidelines or laws will need to be enacted. One thing was certain, however. As long as there are people against abortion, fetal cell transplants for individuals with Parkinson's disease or any other illness will remain a controversial and emotionally charged issue.

CHAPTER 5

Coping

Hearing that you have Parkinson's disease is never easy. Think about it—someone is told that he or she has an incurable degenerative brain disorder. While the ailment isn't fatal, the person won't get any better. Furthermore, as the disease progresses and the individual continues to use medication, it's likely that the drugs won't remain as effective.

How a person reacts to such a diagnosis will probably reflect the way that individual has dealt with unsettling situations in the past. Perhaps the patient knew something was wrong even before seeing the physician. The unexplainable symptoms that seem to worsen with time often cause patients to suspect something serious. Yet when a physician actually labels the condition, reactions vary.

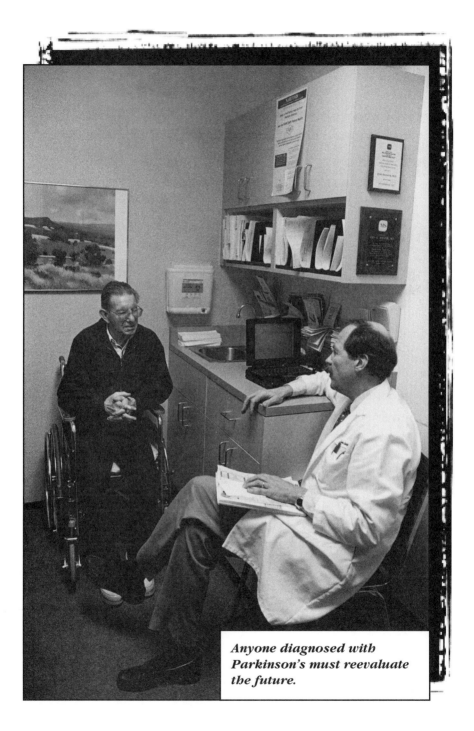

Anyone diagnosed with Parkinson's must reevaluate the future.

Some people deny that anything is really wrong and refuse to even think about Parkinson's disease and the impact it may have on their life and family. Others blame their doctor, claiming that they've been misdiagnosed. Such individuals may then seek other medical opinions, hoping to eventually find someone who'll agree with them. Still others will try to read up on the illness to learn as much as they can about the symptoms and possible solutions.

Hopefully, as the patient and the family come to accept Parkinson's disease as a reality, they'll begin the important task of reevaluating the future. The individual will need to take a long hard look at whether or not he or she will be able to continue to work, and if so, for how long. If the patient has always wanted to go on a special trip with his or her family, they may decide to take it before the person becomes increasingly debilitated. Financial planning strategies for the family may need to be reassessed as well.

Adjusting to Parkinson's disease can also include finding ways to bypass some of the small everyday obstacles presented by the illness. A volunteer at the Los Altos (California) Parkinson's Support Group in conjunction with the Parkinson's Institute devised the following tips "To Make Life Easier" for people with Parkinson's disease.

- An electric toothbrush makes good oral hygiene easier.

- To get the best results from their medication, people with Parkinson's disease may want to discuss adjusting the times they take their prescription drugs with their physicians. In some cases it may be best not to take certain drugs after six or seven in the evening, as some medications tend to keep people awake. When reviewing their medication history with the doctor, it's also a good idea to bring along all their drugs in the original containers. This helps to ensure accuracy.

- Since drug costs vary at different pharmcies, it's helpful to do an informal price check every so often. Frequently, ordering drugs through mail-order services affords even greater savings.

- In instances where Parkinson's disease has made someone's handwriting illegible, a plastic lettering guide or stencil can make a big difference.

- People with Parkinson's disease who experience foot cramps may find it helpful to step on a large smooth rock and press down to straighten out their foot. They may also find it useful to have someone gently step on their foot to spread their toes. Participating in an exercise class both

PD patients may need special aids around the home to help them with daily activities—such as this support for getting out of bed.

for exercise and to socialize can be important in maintaining mobility and a healthy mental outlook.

- People with PD should avoid alcoholic beverages as these can interfere with some types of anti-Parkinson's medications as well as disrupt their sleep. They should also pass up foods that interact adversely with their medications. Numerous people with Parkinson's disease have problems with beverages or dishes that contain caffeine or are high in sugar.

- People with Parkinson's disease can "work" on their voices to make themselves more understandable by "using a lot of air" and "forcing it through." Singing in the shower, or anywhere else for that matter, is also suggested to keep their voices in good shape.

- An occasional massage can soothe muscles that are sore due to Parkinson's disease. Putting leather balm on car seats makes sliding in and out of the vehicle easier. Keeping a plastic bag on the car seat can make someone with PD more comfortable when changing positions in the seat itself.

- People with Parkinson's disease who encounter problems sleeping comfortably in their beds might find resting in a recliner more comfortable. These can be purchased in extra-large and extra-long sizes.

- Getting out of a low chair can sometimes be difficult for someone with PD. Therefore, it's wise to avoid such seats.

- Inexpensive tapes simulating the sound of raindrops, a waterfall, or a fan blowing can be helpful to those with PD who have trouble falling asleep. Trying different sizes and shapes of pillows can also make a difference.

- Swimming and stretching in the shallow portion of a warm pool is often an excellent activity for people with Parkinson's disease.

Also helpful to both individuals with Parkinson's disease and their families are the many PD support groups throughout the country. Usually led by a health care professional, these groups give useful information as well as provide people with an opportunity to see how others in similar situations have coped with Parkinson's.

In addition, support groups can be good fundraising sources for PD research efforts. Each year, the Northeast Kansas Parkinson's Association in Topeka sponsors a "Geranium Bonanza" for this pur-

PD patients and their families can find guidance, support, and advice at PD support groups, which are located throughout the country.

pose. Members take sales orders for the brightly colored plants from their friends, neighbors, and acquaintances. Six weeks later, the geraniums are picked up by the customers at a designated central location. The Marine Corps League and local Boy Scouts serve as volunteers to carry out the geraniums to the buyers' cars. With about one hundred and fifty steady customers and $4,000 earned in gross sales, the Geranium Bonanza has been a profitable venture. To further boost profits, the group is now sending out promotional flyers with order forms to neighboring areas.

The Topeka group has also embarked on another successful fund-raiser. It sells walking sticks (canes) specifically designed for people with Parkinson's disease. In four years, more than $10,000 worth of walking sticks have been sold.

Through support groups and related organizations, family members can learn new strategies for caring for their loved ones while still pursuing fulfilling lives of their own.

This is important since the illness's progression causes significant changes in a person's daily activities or living arrangements. In some parts of the country, adult day care is an alternative when a person with Parkinson's disease should not be home alone during the day. Usually these centers provide nutritious meals, appropriate recreational activities, field trips, music, and art therapy as well as a break from the isolation many people with Parkinson's disease experience. Some centers also offer speech and physical therapy.

Besides caring for the person who has Parkinson's disease, it's important that the caregiver have adequate support. Often, the ill person's spouse or grown child assumes this role. But either way, someone who may already be overburdened with other duties must now see to the needs of an ill family member.

It's crucial to remember that just about everyone in the family can help the main caregiver in some way. Many young people have found it rewarding to assist a grandparent who has Parkinson's disease or to take over chores for a parent who is involved in the ill person's care. Many of these teens claim that being involved made them feel as though they were part of the team and it meant a great deal to them.

There are many things a caregiver can do to ease his or her role. Texas Tech University Health Sciences Center offers some examples:

- Give family members or friends specific suggestions on how to be helpful. For example, going to the grocery store or post office, bringing a meal, or sitting with the loved one for an afternoon or evening.

- Maintain your health. You are more capable of helping another if you care for yourself too. Continue to go to ... social activities that are meaningful to you. Carry on traditions that are comforting (holiday decorating, special Sunday meals, etc.).

- Treat yourself to something every week (lunch out, a movie, a special purchase, etc.).

- Consider changing your routine. Add new approaches to your daily activities.

- Find a "hermit" spot where you can spend some quiet time.

- Acknowledge that feelings of anger, frustration, and fatigue are normal for caregivers, especially those in a long-term role.

- Know the difference between "talking out" problems with an understanding listener to relieve tension, and chronic complaining that only reinforces negative feelings.

- Learn to say "no." Your "yes" will mean more.

- Consider the companionship of a house pet. A mild mannered dog or cat can offer love and comfort.

- Hire someone to help around the house. Even two hours of service a week can give you a needed break.

- Talk with a nurse or social worker about ways to manage problem behaviors of your loved one. Area home healthcare agencies can send an R.N. to visit your home to suggest ways of coping. Inquire about help through the office of Area Agency of Aging, R.S.V.P. (Retired Senior Volunteer Program), or other community social service organizations. Look into joining a local support group. You may share common feelings and suggestions with others in similar situations.

• Recognize when you've done all you can. Deciding to seek additional help whether through home-care services or institutional care can be difficult. Talking with a discharge planner or social worker can help you clarify your needs and make appropriate choices.[1]

In the end, family members usually see that even though Parkinson's disease may somewhat change the way they relate to a loved one who is ill, it can't lessen the depth of feeling that has existed between them through the years.

As one young woman said of her grandfather who has Parkinson's disease,

"When I tell Grandpa how much I love him, tears come to his eyes. . . . He's had Parkinson's disease for about eight years . . . It hurts knowing that Grandpa can no

By facing the challenges of PD together, many families have grown closer.

longer live the kind of lifestyle he's been used to, but I don't think about the things that can never be again. I concentrate on today and today only ....Grandpa is full of life and still needs the love I feel in my heart for him.... It doesn't bother me to have to shave Grandpa or bring him some tissues when he gets a little choked up being with his family.

Without Grandpa, there wouldn't be a family.... And how could I ever stop loving the man who's given me so much to be thankful for? Parkinson's disease creates a handicap for those who suffer from it, but it has no effect on the love you share with the people who are dear to you, like my Grandpa."[2]

End Notes

CHAPTER 1

1. David L. Carroll, *Living With Parkinson's;A Guide for the Patient and Caregiver,* (New York: HarperCollins Publishers, 1992), 26.

2. "Study on Minorities With Parkinson's Disease Gets Endorsement From Muhammad Ali," *Jet,* October 14, 1996, 34

3. Ibid., 7.

4. Ibid.

5. National Institute of Neurological Disorders and Stroke, *Hope Through Research; Parkinson's Disease,* (Bethesda, Maryland: National Institutes of Health, 1994), 8.

CHAPTER 2

1. David L. Carroll, *Living With Parkinson's;A Guide for the Patient and Caregiver*, (New York: HarperCollins Publishers, 1992), 34.

2. Thomas L. Delvanco, M.D., "A 61-Year-Old Man With Parkinson's Disease; 1 Year Later," *JAMA*, October 9, 1996, 1171.

3. L. Seachrest, "Tranquilizers Mimic Parkinson's Symptoms," *Science News*, August 5, 1995, 86.

4. Ibid.

5. Ibid.

6. David L. Carroll, 38.

7. Ibid., 40

8. Charles Huseman, "Comments From the Spouse of a Parkinson Patient," *Coping With Parkinson's Disease*, (Staten Island, New York: The American Parkinson Disease Association, Inc., 1986), 14-15.

CHAPTER 3

1. Rose Wichman, R.P.T., *Be Active;A Suggested Exercise Program for People With Parkinson's Disease*, (Staten Island, New York:The American Parkinson Disease Association, Inc., 1977), 2.

CHAPTER 4

1. Deborah Franklin, "The Parkinson's Predicament," *Health*, May/June 1996, 62.

2. Ibid., 63.

3. Ibid.

4. Michael Weill, "Moment of Truth," *People Weekly,* July 31, 1995, 38.

5. Ibid.

6. Jeff Goldberg, "Fetal Attraction," *Discover,* July 1994, 90.

7. Ibid.

8. Ibid.

9. Ibid.

10. Ibid., 91.

11. Ibid.

12. Ibid.

13. Ibid.

14. Ibid., 93

15. Ibid.

16. Ibid.

17. J. Travis, "Pig Cells Used for Parkinson's Disease," *Science News,* October 7, 1995, 230.

18. Ibid.

CHAPTER 5

1. Texas Tech University Health Sciences Center, "Suggestions to Help Caregivers Sustain Their Emotional and Physical Energies so They Can Continue to Givethe Best Care to their Loved One," *Coping With Parkinson's Disease,* (Staten Island, New York: The American Parkinson Disease Association, Inc., 1986), 28.

2. Joyce H. Levin, "Parkinson's Disease Doesn't Stop my Love for Grandpa," *Coping With Parkinson's Disease,* (Staten Island, New York: The American Parkinson Disease Association, Inc., 1986), 11.

Glossary

bradykinesia — slowness of movement; a gradual loss of spontaneous movement

corpus striatum — the portion of brain that helps to regulate movement or motor activities

dementia — a loss of mental or intellectual abilities including impairment of judgment and memory

dopamine — a neurotransmitter or chemical messenger in the brain which sends impulses from one cell to another. People with Parkinson's disease are deficient in dopamine.

dyskinesia — involuntary movements of the limbs and other body parts which can take the form of twitching, nodding, and jerking. Dyskinesia frequently occurs in people with Parkinson's disease who have been taking large quantities of levodopa for extended periods of time.

festination — the tendency of people with Parkinson's disease to take short quick steps forward

idiopathic or primary Parkinson's disease — the type of Parkinson's disease for which there is no known cause. This type of Parkinson's disease differs from other types of PD such as toxin-induced parkinsonism, arteriosclerotic parkinsonism, *parkinsonism*-dementia complex of Guam, and others.

rigidity — stiffness in the limbs and muscles; a common Parkinson's disease symptom

substantia nigra — a portion of the brain where the brain chemical dopamine is normally produced. In people with Parkinson's disease, nerve cells in this area of the brain die or become damaged.

Further Readings

Atwood, Glenna Wotton. *Living With Parkinson's;
An Inspirational Informative Guide for
Parkinsonians and Their Loved Ones.* New
York: John Wiley & Sons, Inc., 1991.

Check, William A. *Alzheimer's Disease.* New York:
Chelsea House, 1989.

Dauphin, Sue. *Parkinson's Disease; The Mystery,
the Search, and the Promise.* Tequesta, FL: Pixel
Press, 1992.

Durrett, Deanne. *Organ Transplants.* San Diego, CA:
Lucent Books, 1993.

Duvoisin, Roger C. *Parkinson's Disease; A Guide
for the Patient and Family.* New York: Raven
Press, 1991.

Facklam, Margery. *Healing Drugs; The History of Pharmacology.* New York: Facts On File, 1992.

Kusinitz, Marc. *Poisons and Toxins.* New York: Chelsea House, 1993.

Landau, Elaine. *Alzheimer's Disease.* Danbury, CT: Franklin Watts, Inc., 1996.

Leinwand, Gerald. *Transplants; Today's Medical Miracles.* Danbury, CT: Franklin Watts, 1992.

McGoon, Dwight C. *The Parkinson's Handbook.* New York: Norton, 1990.

O'Neil, Karen E. *Health and Medical Projects For Young Scientists.* Danbury, CT: Franklin Watts, Inc., 1993.

Silverstein, Alvin and Virginia. *World of the Brain.* New York: Morrow, 1986.

Organizations

THE AMERICAN PARKINSON DISEASE ASSOCIATION, INC.
1250 Hylan Boulevard, Suite 4B
Staten Island, New York 10305-1946
800-223-2732

APDA West Coast Office
15000 Ventura Boulevard, Suite 384
Sherman Oaks, California 91403
800-908-2732

APDA Washington D.C. Office
807 South Alfred Street, #2
Alexandria, Virginia 22314
800-684-2732

NATIONAL PARKINSON FOUNDATION, INC.
  National Headquarters
    Bob Hope Parkinson Research Center
    Parkinson Diagnostic Rehabilitation Treatment
      Center & Care Institute
    1501 N.W. 9th Avenue, Bob Hope Road
    Miami, Florida 33136-1494
    Telephone: 305-547-6666
    Toll Free Nat'l: 800-327-4545, Fax: 305-243-4403
    Internet e-mail: mailbox@hpf.med.miami.edu
    World Wide Web: http://www.parkinson.org

  California Office
    National Parkinson Foundation, Inc.
    15840 Ventura Boulevard, Suite 215
    Encino, California 91436
    Telephone: 818-981-2233, Fax: 818-981-7392
    Toll Free Nat'l: 800-522-8855
    Toll Free in California: 800-400-8448

  New York Office
    National Parkinson Foundation, Inc.
    10 Union Square East, Suite 2R
    New York, New York 10003
    Telephone: 212-844-8485

  Washington Office
    National Parkinson Foundation, Inc.
    1250 24th Street, N.W., Suite 300
    Washington, D.C. 20037
    Telephone: 202-466-0550
    Fax: 202-466-0585

Parkinson's Disease Foundation
William Black Medical Research Building
710 West 168th Street
New York, New York 10032
800-457-6676

The Parkinson's Institute
1170 Morse Avenue
Sunnyvale, California 94089
408-734-2800 (Ext. 644 for Outreach)
800-655-2273

Parkinson's Support Groups of America
11376 Cherry Hill Road, #204
Beltsville, Maryland 20705
301-937-1545

United Parkinson Foundation
833 West Washington Blvd.
Chicago, Illinois 60607
312-733-1893

Index

Mobility, exercises for, 52-54, *53*

Monane, Mark, 29

Mood swings, 20

Motor system disorder, 9

Movement, slowness of, 7, 8, 10-11, 13, 51
See also Bradykinesia
MPTP, 13-14, 31, 46, 49-50

Multiple system atrophy (Shy-Drager syndrome), 32

National Institute of Health (NIH), 15, 64, 70, 71, 74

National Institute of Mental Health, 49

National Institute of Neurological Disorders and Stroke (NINDS), 22, 49

National Parkinson Foundation, 23

Nausea, 42, 44, 46, 48, 51

Network of European CNS Transplantation and Restoration (NECTAR), 75

Neurophysiologist, 60-61

Neurotransmitter, dopamine, 18-19, 40

Neurotransplantation, 75-76

Nightmares, 28, 46

Occurrences of PD, 22-23

Olanow, C. Warren, 70-71

Olson, Lars, 49-50

On-off effect, of levadopa, 43-44

Operations, 56-77, *58*

Pacemaker (brain implant), 48

Pallidal Stimulation, 57

Pallidotomy, 57, 59-63

Parkinson, James, 13

Parkinsonism-Dementia Complex of Guam, 31

Pergolide, 46

Personal accounts. *See* Accounts, personal

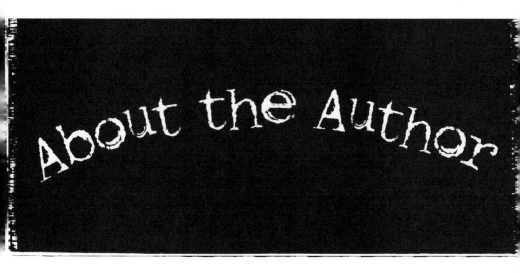

About the Author

Popular author Elaine Landau worked as a newspaper reporter, an editor, and a youth services librarian before becoming a full-time writer. She has written more than seventy nonfiction books for young people, including *We Have AIDS* and *Alzheimer's Disease*. Ms. Landau, who has a bachelor's degree in English and journalism from New York University and a master's degree in library and information science from Pratt Institute, lives in Florida with her husband and son.